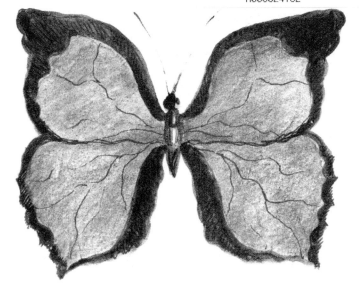

Believe 2

A poetry collection by John F Connor

Fantastic Books Publishing Edition

ISBN: 978-1-909163-54-6

Cover Design by Paula Ann Murphy

Internal Illustrations by Jolanta Dziok

License Notes

This book is licensed for your personal enjoyment only. This book may not be re-sold or given away to other people. If you would like to share this book with another person, please purchase an additional copy for each recipient. If you're reading this book and did not purchase it, or it was not purchased for your use only, then please purchase your own copy. Thank you for respecting the hard work of this author.

About John

John Connor was born in 1964 and has been writing poetry since he was sixteen. Following the death of his Mother and Father, John noticed that his poetry had changed. He wrote to give himself comfort and when he shared his words with others found his poems also gave comfort to them.

Now, with thousands of followers on Facebook and a regular spot writing poetry for a grief management site called

'Healing Hugs', John is surprised at his sudden rise to fame. His work has also appeared on the 'Words of Wisdom' site which currently has over a million followers!

A down to earth family man who dreams of going to America due to his love of 1950s music, John wants his poetry to touch the hearts and souls of those lost in grief.

This is his second collection and he continues to hope that his poetry will inspire and comfort you in your daily life.

John has agreed to donate 10% of the proceeds of his first collection to the St Helena Hospice in Colchester, UK, a charity close to John's heart.

10% of the proceeds of this collection will be donated to the grief management site 'Healing Hugs' who do wonderful work helping people all over the world deal with feelings of pain and loss.

Dedication

Along with each and every one of you reading this right now, I dedicate this to the people in my life that have shaped me into the man I am today.

To my mother and father, uncle Tony Bennett, uncle Jimmy Gant and most of all to my brave wife .

I hope you enjoy this collection of poems.

'I have lived with grief all my life. That's why my poems come straight from the heart. The words just enter my head.'

- John Connor

CONTENTS

Fight

Sometimes you have to fight a battle

But you fear you are on your own

Then others come from everywhere

You don't have to fight alone

For in your darkest hour

When you don't know what to do

True friends will raise an army

To help you to get through

They will come from everywhere

Devoted friends and family, strong and true

When the call goes out

They are there for you

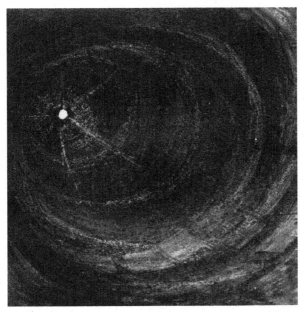

Tears of a clown

Sometimes a smile hides a secret

Laughter hides the tears

Not wanting others to know

Of the sorrow or the fears

Tears of a clown hide the pain

So others cannot see

Someone who is in a place

That they don't want to be

Happy on the outside

But the pain lies deep within

Trying to fight their demons

Is a battle they must win

Depression is an illness
It's not a state of mind
They need a lot of love
People who are kind
For it's a lonely battle
That can cut a life short
This person needs your help
Encouragement and support

A friend

A friend will make you smile
Whenever you are blue
A friend knows you inside out
A friend knows what to do
A friend has time to spare
When you are on your own
A friend will always check on you
Or ring you on the phone
A friend will never let you down
Or walk past you in the street
A friend will cross the road
Just so you can meet

A friend will always forgive
No matter what you do
Because I have a friend like this
And that dear friend is you

Butterfly Kisses

Don't cry for me; please don't be sad

Hold on to the memories of the times we both had

Don't dwell on dark thoughts; hold on tight to your wishes

Sending you hugs and butterfly kisses

I walk beside you; I am there all day long

I am right here but you think I am gone

You don't see me but I can see you

Whatever the problems I will help get you through

I am the wind in your hair, the sand in your toes

Butterfly kisses that you feel on your nose
I am with you at sunrise and through to sunset
That you cannot see me is my one regret
I sit right beside you when you are sad
As you look through the photos of times we both had
I watch you sleeping, I hold you so tight
Before I go I kiss you goodnight
I will watch over you from heaven above
Forever you will be my one true love
Hold on to your dreams and all your wishes
Sending you hugs and butterfly kisses

I never left you

Wherever you go
Whatever you do
Though you don't see me
I'm right there with you
Though you don't see me
Though you don't hear
I know in your heart
You know I am near
You speak to me often
Sometimes you cry
As you look at old pictures
And ask yourself why
But I will be there
To help with the pain
For I know the truth
I will see you again

Graveyard

I watch you when you visit

Sometimes you stay for hours

Telling me about your life

While tenderly laying flowers

You tell how you miss me

And how you love me so

You want answers to questions

You ask me why I had to go

On birthdays you bring cards

At Christmas you bring them too

Every time you visit

I am there with you

When you sit upon the bench
So much you don't understand
I am sitting right beside you
Sometimes I hold your hand
My body may lie there
But I'm in heaven up above
Free from all my pain
Wrapped in peace and love

The father's child

I remember my father saying

As he sat me upon his knee

How he had messed up his life

And would live his dreams through me

How he would always be there

Through good times and through bad

How he would try to give me

All the things he never had

For I am my father's child

A bond that cannot be broken

Who guides me through this life

With wise words he has spoken

For I am my father's child

That is the way it will always be

When others let me down

He was always there for me

My young years were so happy
I remember them with pleasure
I knew that he was special
Our love you could not measure
He always spent time with me
Days so full of laughter
That stay inside my memory
For now and ever after
Teenage years were hard
I caused him lots of grief
He could see beyond the fear
He knew what was underneath
When people broke my heart
He told taught me not to worry
Taught me that life is a gift
One too good to hurry
I thought he would live forever
But God took him to rest
But to have him as a father
I knew that I had been blessed
I wish to hear him laugh
I wish I could see him smile
I wish that God above
Had left him here a while

How can I walk in your shoes?
How can I make things right?
How can I live without you?
I am crying every night
For a child can love its father
But some words are left unsaid
I wish I'd told you while you were here
So much was left unsaid
Place flowers at his graveside
My new-born on my arm
I will be just like my father
Protecting mine from harm
I will teach the words you told me
I will try to be a guide guide
To have you for my father
Just fills me up with pride
I keep a picture of us
It hangs proud upon my wall
You were always there for me
Picked me up when I did fall
One day we will be together
I know what I will do
I will hold you in my arms
And say, Father, I love you

Must I

Must I go through life
With an empty heart?
How do I face tomorrow
Now we are apart?
I know if you were here
Just what you would say
Pull yourself together
Don't throw your life away
Yes, it won't be easy
But that's the way it has to be
Enjoy what you have left
One day you'll be with me

Life

It does not do to dwell on death
But live your life with every breath
Seeking answers to questions no one can give
This is your life, get out and live
Never waste a single day
Don't take to heart what others say
This is your life to shape and hone
We enter and we leave alone
Search in your heart and you will see
There is so much more to you and me
When loved ones pass don't sit and mourn
Their time did come, their souls reborn

One day when the time is right
You will close your eyes and see the light
A wondrous journey you will take
Leading you to heaven's gate
So live your life and please don't worry
We all get there one day, so what's the hurry
There is more to life than we will ever know
Just sit back and enjoy the show

My Resolution

My new year's resolution

Is to be happy and not sad

Not to dwell on what I have lost

But to remember what I had

Not to ponder on what might have been

Not to give in to grief

To search inside my soul

To believe what's underneath

To live my life and live it full

To take on whatever comes my way

Not to plan too far ahead

But live life for the day

To believe that I can do things

I have never done before
To realize you have not gone
You're just behind another door
To know that you will guide me
Forever walk by my side
To show you I am strong
That I still have my pride
I will make you proud
And show I've nothing to fear
Though I may not see you
I often feel you near

My right to mourn

How can I tell my heart
That you have gone away?
I want to make things right
But don't know what to say
I am lonely and sad
I cannot believe you have gone
But others tell me to get over it
They say I must move on
But they don't know how I feel
They would not know where to start
One minute I was happy
Then my world was ripped apart

23

Yes I need to mourn
And to do it my own way
To listen to my heart
And not what others say
Yes there will be dark times
Yes I will be sad
It will hurt me for a while
When I remember what we had
But time will heal my heart
Time will ease the sorrow
It may not be today
It may not be tomorrow
Yes there will be tears
I may scream and shout
I cannot lock the pain away
I have to let it out
True friends will stick by me
Others may walk away
True friends will hold my hand
And listen to what I have to say
It's my right to mourn
And to learn to deal with grief
It's not what you see on the outside
But the way I feel underneath

No shame

There is no shame in crying
There is no shame in feeling sad
There is no shame in grieving
For the loved ones you once had
There is no shame in hurting
There is no shame in sorrow
Grief has no time limit
Could be today, could be tomorrow
There is no shame in silence
There is no shame in tears
It may take a while
Days or months or years
Remember we all are different
No one grieves the same
But however long it takes
Remember there is no shame

Maybe tomorrow

Maybe tomorrow my pain will cease

Maybe tomorrow my heart will find peace

Maybe tomorrow I will get my life back

Maybe tomorrow the sky won't be black

Maybe tomorrow I will cry my last tear

Maybe tomorrow I will have nothing to fear

Maybe tomorrow my sadness will go

Maybe tomorrow 'cause you just never know

Wherever

Wherever I go
Whatever I do
Deep in my heart
There's a longing for you
I long for your touch
I long for your smile
I long to hold you
If just for a while

Don't tell me

Don't tell me to get over it

Don't tell me to move on

Don't tell me time's a healer

Don't tell me to be strong

I need my time to grieve

I need my time alone

No one else can rush me

I need to do this on my own

Yes. it may take a while

Yes. it may take years

Yes. I may shout and scream

And cry a lot of tears

But only when I'm ready

Not because you tell me so

For when the time is right

I will be the one to know

Letter to mum

I see you mum but you don't see me

But I am always there

I watch you when you are sleeping

I gently stroke your hair

I hug you when you cry

I kiss you when you are sad

I sit beside you as you look through photos

Of the good times we both had

I often say I love you

In words you cannot hear

I know sometimes you feel me

You know that I am near

So don't cry mum, I love you
I have not gone forever
Just watching over you in heaven
Till the time to be together
It is hard to watch you suffer
Knowing there is nothing I can do
Our bond cannot be broken
I will help to pull you through
Death is not the darkness
Death is the everlasting light
Keeping me from harm
Until the time is right

I am ok

Just a little letter
I just wanted to say
Everything is fine
And I got here ok
I made it to heaven
This place is really great
Family there to meet me
They were waiting by the gate
I am young again
No illness and no pain
Things I could not do on earth
I now can do again
This place is beautiful

I feel like I've come home
There are waterfalls and flowers
And green fields where I roam
Please don't worry about me
For I am in good care
And when the time is right
I will meet you there
Enjoy the life you have
Cherish every single day
Just wanted you to know
That I got here ok

Letter to heaven

Pen to paper

Words from my heart

So much to say

But where do I start?

I really love you

And miss you every day

My heart was broken

When angels took you that day

But I have the memories

Of all the good times we had

They make me smile

On days I feel sad

I thank you for the times

That we shared together
The next time I see you
We will be together forever
Now rest in peace my darling
May angels wrap you in love
As you sing with the seraphim
In heaven above
This is not goodbye
Just a parting in time
I will be yours forever
You will forever be mine
When I get to heaven
You'll be the first one I see
For that will be the moment
He gives you back to me

The light

I close my eyes and see the light

Does not hurt but very bright

I feel happy, content and free from pain

Then I hear someone say my name

They say that I must go away

It's not my time, I cannot stay

Your life's not over, you have much to do

He has other plans for you

Live a full life, have no fear

Heaven will always be waiting here

Believe in heaven; do not fear death

Enjoy your life with every breath

The gift of life is just a test

To live and learn and do your best

To grow to love to cry to care

To guide to help to give to share

Answers

Wish I had the answers
To all the questions that you have
Wish I could make you happy
Whenever you are sad
Wish I could go to heaven
And bring a loved one back to you
If I could find a way
Then that's what I would do
Wish I knew life's meaning
What it was all about
I have tried for many hours
But I can't figure it out

But if you look around you
I am sure that you will see
That life is such a gift
Given to you and me
Don't ponder on the what ifs
Live life for the day
To ponder too long on deep thoughts
Is to throw your life away
Remember that life is for living
So go out and grab your chances
Life asks all the questions
Death holds all the answers

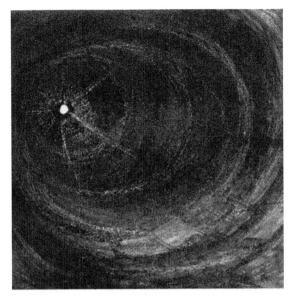

The Journey

I am going on a journey
I may be gone a while
Don't remember me with sadness
But laughter and a smile
I am going where the angels sing
Where pain and suffering cease
Where I can put my load down
And find a little peace
I am meeting many others
Don't fear, I am not alone
There are blue skies and rivers
And green fields where I roam
But I will never be far away

Though we may be apart
And if you ever need me
You will find me in your heart
Please don't grieve for me
I have not gone forever
When the time is right
We will be together
I will always watch you
Wherever you may be
I will leave you little signs
So you will know it's me

I Know

Whatever I do
Wherever I go
There is one thing
I want you to know
From the moment I wake
Till last thing at night
I know in my heart
That you are alright
I know you're in heaven
I know that you see
I am thinking of you
As you look down on me

You know that I love you
You know that I care
Though I cannot see you
I just know you are there
I know in my heart
I believe in the greater
This is not goodbye
It's just see you later

It's hard

I find it hard this time of year
Hard to believe that you're not here
But I am brave and wear a smile
Giving in is not my style
I know that you are not too far
A butterfly and shining star
Body gone but your soul is free
I know that you are here with me
Sending you hugs and lots of kisses
All my love and my best wishes
I will not cry, I will not grieve
I have my faith and I believe

I believe in heaven above
A place of peace and hope and love
Where families are reunited
When life is done and we are invited
Heaven's true life forever goes on
Believe in this and you'll stay strong

To lose a child

To lose a child very young
When their life had just begun
Is the greatest pain I know
Not understanding why they had to go
The special bond they make with you
Let's you know they have souls too
And every soul will live forever
One day you will be together
No one knows the reason why
Why a child had to die
Heaven has a special place
Where babes are loved and they are safe
A place of peace, a place of love
A wondrous place in heaven above

Daddy's Girl

I was proud to be a daddy's girl
I say this with my heart
For a girl can rely on her father
Right from her life's start
My daddy was my hero
A giant in my eye
When he put me on his shoulders
I swear I could touch the sky
I'd sit and wait by the window
To see him come up the path
Then run into his arms
My, how we used to laugh
I knew that he would protect me
I felt safe when he was about

If he didn't like my boyfriends
He was quick to throw them out
When a girl is feeling blue
Or just a little sad
The problems just fade away
With a cuddle from her dad
Some men let me down
Some men made me sad
Only one man a girl can rely upon
And that man is her dad
I really miss you daddy
But our bond is as strong as ever
You watch over me in heaven
Till the day we are together
And when I get to heaven's gate
I know what I will do
Your will be there with open arms
And I will run to you

Sometimes

Sometimes my mind just slips away
With memories of another day
When sun was out and sky was blue
Holding your hand and walking with you
Birds were singing grass was green
Sitting together by a clear blue stream
Laughing happy carefree and young
Like our lives had just begun
Happy days we shared together
Live in my memories forever and ever
You may be gone but you're not far
In the night sky you're a new-born star

Watching me from heaven above
A place of wonder peace and love
Knowing we will meet again
Will help me get through the pain
Our memories I have to treasure
Will stay with me now and forever
Someday when the time is right
You will be waiting in the light

Lonely heart

Lonely heart why are you blue?
Lonely heart what can I do?
Lonely heart what can I say?
Someone you love has gone away
Lonely heart please don't be sad
Remember all the times you had
Lonely heart I feel your pain
If you believe you'll meet again
Lonely heart please don't cry
Lonely heart it's not goodbye
Just moved on to somewhere greater
It's not goodbye but see you later

A place

I dream of a beautiful place
Where pain and suffering end
Where age and time cease to matter
And everyone is your friend
A place that has all the answers
To all the questions you ever had
Where everyone's souls fly free
Where nobody is sad
This place waits for all of us
When the time is right

Just travel through the darkness
Until you reach the light
Where lost loves are reunited
And families are put back together
Where death has no place
For everyone lives forever
Enjoy the gift of life
Do not waste one single day
Our loved ones walk beside us
They never go away

Graveside

Do not stand at my graveside

As if to say goodbye

I am still here

I did not die

I stand beside you

But you don't see

I give you signs

To show it's me

I see, I touch

I smell, I feel

Everything they say

About heaven is real

I see your tears
I hear you sigh
But please don't ever
Say goodbye
Just trust my words
And carry on
I am still here
I have not gone

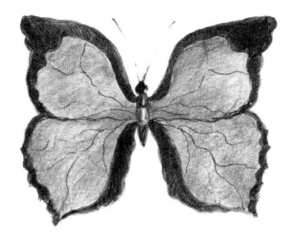

There is

There is black, there is white

There is day, there is night

There is weak, there is strong

There is right, there is wrong

There is good, there is bad

There is happy, there is sad

There is peace, there is war

There is less, there is more

There is hate, there is love

There is below, there is above

There is light, there is dark

There is stop, there is start

There is loss, there is hope
There is cotton, there is rope
There is age, there is youth
There is falsehood, there is truth
There is run, there is walk
There is silence, there is talk
There is a converse to everything you do
The choice you make is up to you

My wall

I have built a wall around me

So others cannot get in

I need to take it down

But don't know where to begin

One brick at a time

But at a steady pace

Only when I am ready

To come out and show my face

I need time on my own

To help me cope with sorrow

It may not be today

It may not be tomorrow

Only I will know

When the time is right

This is a battle

That only I can fight

A summer's day

As I walk along on a hot summer's day
I let my mind just drift away
To a place I like to be
All alone myself and me
A little time to call my own
To think things through
In peace alone
To clear my head of all that's wrong
At peace as I just walk along
Stop for a while and feel the breeze
Hear it whistle through the trees

65

Watch the birds as they fly up high
See the clouds go rolling by
At one with nature, all at peace
We all need time to have release
We need time to think things through
To clear our minds to know what to do
To appreciate just what we have
To know that life is not so bad

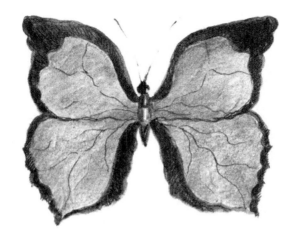

Never give in

Never give in

Never surrender

You are a fighter

You just need to remember

Yes, things will test you

Yes, things will go wrong

But it's just a test

To make us grow strong

If you give up the fight

How will you ever know

What you could become

And how far you could grow?

You

Wherever I go
Whatever I do
My thoughts always
Go back to you
The times we shared
The fun we had
Make me feel
A little sad
I hold onto
The memory
A special time
Just you and me
I won't forget
In passing time

One I lost

Who once was mine

My pain may heal

May take a while

For tear drops

To become a smile

Breaks my heart

To know you've gone

But for others

I must be strong

But I know

Don't ask me why

It's see you later

It's not goodbye

My childhood home

When I visit our old house

A chill runs down my spine

As memories take me back

To another time

I can see where father used to sit

And watch his old TV

While mother was in the kitchen

Making us our tea

I can hear sister playing records

Volume at full blast

Just like a time machine

Taking me to my past

God they were such happy days
Memories still linger on
Time moves oh so fast
Where have the years gone?
Playing in the garden
Riding on my bike
Fishing by a river
Trying to fly a kite
Now the house is empty
But the memories remain
Just by standing here
I'm in that time again
Whenever I am down
I always visit here
I feel my mum and dad
Are so very near
I did not know it then
It made me what I am today
Memories stay forever
They never fade away

Angel On My Shoulder

An angel on my shoulder
Who is with me each day
Who's always there to guide me
To show me the right way
Angel on my shoulder
Whose love is pure and true
Who never leaves my side
No matter what I do
Angel on my shoulder
Sent from up above
A heavenly soul so pure
Heart filled with peace and love

Angel on my shoulder
Who helps to keep me strong
Who understands that sometimes
In life I get things wrong
Angel on my shoulder
Who does not judge what I do
Who knows when I need help
Is there to get me through

Angel On My Bed

An angel was sitting on my bed
I said to the angel, Am I dead?
No, she said. You have nothing to fear
That is not the reason why I am here
I have been sent to watch over you
In times of trouble I guide you through
But I know you don't believe in me
So here I am for you to see
Your loved ones past want you to know
Just how much they love you so
They asked me to come so you would believe
It hurts them so much to watch you grieve
They want you to be happy safe and free from pain
They said that you will meet again
Now close your eyes, good night God bless
So do you believe in angels? I said YES

Pick a rose

Pick me a rose in heaven

Give it to the one I love

Tell them it's from me

To heaven up above

Tell them that I miss them

Every single day

Tell how my heart was broken

When angels took them away

Tell them that I love them

And the memories will remain

That this is not goodbye

That we will meet again

My christmas prayer

I pray for a world full of peace

Where all wars and conflicts cease

I pray every illness has a cure

That no one suffers anymore

I pray the hungry all get fed

I pray the homeless have a bed

I pray for a world free from fears

Free from sorrow pain and tears

I pray that deserts get some rain

I pray for a world free from pain

I pray all nations get along
I pray the weak will grow strong
I pray we give and do not take
I pray for love instead of hate
So this is my Christmas prayer
I hope my message gets out there

To finish this book, below is a medley of short, inspirational verses by John Connor

I close my eyes and drift away
To memories of a perfect day
A perfect day we spent together
One day I wished would last forever
If I close my eyes I can see your face
I know you are in a special place
Your body dies, your soul flies free
I know you are watching over me
I am waiting on the other side
Until we are together
The next time that I see you
It will be forever

Live your life and live it full
Never dwell on sorrow
Give thanks for today
Look forward to tomorrow

Never give in
Never surrender
You are stronger than this
You just need to remember

When you are feeling really sad
And don't know what to do
Remember behind the darkest clouds
There awaits a sky of blue

Believe in yourself
Not what others say
This is your life
So live it your way

Today I feel happy
Today I feel free
Today I give thanks
For just being me

Publisher's note

When I first met John it was via a telephone meeting about publishing his first collection of poetry 'Believe'. It was clear from that point that this man had something magical about him. We spoke about his inspiration and how he creates his poems and he explained that in most cases he is simply relaxing at home or out in the garden and an unquenchable urge to write overtakes him. He talked about the feeling that these poems would suddenly announce themselves in his head and he simply had to write them down.

He told me that he simply wanted to get his words out to as many people suffering from grief and heartache as he could. John's healing poetry has already been an inspiration for thousands of people, from all backgrounds, from all over the world. His simple, heartfelt style reflects his own personality as a helpful, friendly and wonderful person.

It has been a privilege to publish John's work and to help him get his inspirational poetry out to the world.

I sincerely hope you have enjoyed this, his second collection, and will recommend it to your friends.

Thank you.

Dan Grubb

Fantastic Books Publishing

CPSIA information can be obtained at www.ICGtesting.com
Printed in the USA
LVOW04s1920010515

436906LV00014B/1110/P